My Life on This Planet

A Letter Board Speller's Revolutionary Insights into the Paradox of Autism

LINA HJALMARSSON LYONS

Skyhorse Publishing

Skyhorse Publishing books may be purchased in bulk at special discounts for sales promotion, corporate gifts, fund-raising, or educational purposes. Special editions can also be created to specifications. For details, contact the Special Sales Department, Skyhorse Publishing, 307 Fifth Avenue, 4th Floor, New York, NY 10016 or info@skyhorsepublishing.com.

Visit our website at www.skyhorsepublishing.com.

10 9 8 7 6 5 4 3 2 1

Library of Congress Control Number: 2026946248

Cover design by Brian Peterson
Cover photo credit: Helena Hjalmarsson

Print ISBN: 978-1-5107-8891-6
Ebook ISBN: 978-1-5107-8892-3

Printed in the United States of America

I dedicate this book to my lovely sister Elsa.

Contents

Foreword

BY GEOFFREY SANBORN

I first met Lina in July 2024, at an autism school on the second floor of a strip mall near Paterson, New Jersey. A couple of months earlier, at the request of her sister Elsa, a student of mine at Amherst College, I had agreed to teach a class for Lina and three other mostly nonspeaking college-aged students at the school: Yamaan, Brian, and Jason. I wasn't sure that it was going to work, but Elsa and her mother, Helena, thought that it could, and what they had told me about Lina and the other students had given me the feeling that it was worth trying. So on a hot afternoon, in a small, square room, with lots of traffic noise coming in through the windows, I began by meeting individually with each of the students and their facilitators.

I almost gave up right then. Not because communication was impossible—not at all. In response to my questions, Lina and the other students pointed to letters on a laminated, 8.5-by-11-inch piece of paper, spelling out responses that the facilitators spoke aloud, but that I could follow myself, once I had gotten used to the process. And all four students very clearly wanted to communicate with me, and I wanted very much to do the same, which meant that I could feel, in each case, the stirrings of a nonverbal attunement. But autism is real. Yamaan's autism kept his responses limited and restricted his eye contact; Brian's autism made him break out in loud half-shouts; Jason's mixture of autism and OCD made him repeat phrases that he didn't intend to utter; and Lina's mixture of autism and OCD had the same effect. I saw right away that it would be possible to tutor each of them, but I really didn't know whether we were going to able to meet as a class.

But Helena encouraged me to try anyway. And when we all gathered in the room, something special happened. When I spoke about my plan for the course—recording myself reading short stories, emailing them the recordings, together with questions for them to answer, and then receiving from their facilitators, before class, a transcription of their letter-boarded responses—they were quiet, still, and attentive. A desire to be a part of this process overrode the forces that could have disrupted it. By the time I said, "Goodbye, see you next week," I knew that it was going to work.

I just didn't know how well. After a couple of weeks during which I was gauging the level at which they were responding to the stories and experimenting with ways of integrating those responses into my hour-long lectures—I had sensed that in-class letter-boarding would create anxiety and scatter attention—the class took off. I would begin by talking about that week's story in a way that modeled a relaxed but intense interest in it, and then I would turn to one of the students' responses, reading from it and commenting on it with the same kind of interest. Then, from that vantage point, I would pivot to a relevant aspect of the story. (Getting the responses in advance allowed me to plan this out.) I would then turn to a different student's response, pivot to a different aspect of the story, and so on. I would wrap up by talking about the relationship that I saw between their responses and the qualities of the story that their responses had individually and collectively revealed. There were always distractions and disruptions, especially when the stories had been upsetting in some way. But they were so interested in each other's responses, and in what I had to say about their own responses, that the classes held together. A feeling of change was in the air.

That fall, Lina and Jason audited an introductory literature course that I was teaching at Amherst. Most of their participation was online—they contributed responses to the same discussion forum that my Amherst students used—but each of them came to a couple of classes and each of them gave an in-class presentation at the end of the semester. When Lina came for her presentation, she visited me in my office first, and with Helena facilitating, we communicated for a little while.

"How do you feel about coming to class?" I asked.

"I am so yearning for connections," Lina typed (the word may sound strange, but it's the best way of describing it—the alphabet on the laminated sheet of paper is just a different kind of keyboard). "I have a hole in my heart in terms of connections." As she touched the letters, she occasionally said them out loud.

I said something or other in response, and Lina typed, "I am so in alignment with Elsa and I am so sad at not being able to s-t-t-u"—she broke off, and then continued—"study." She paused again, and then went back to it. "My school is about mastering the body, not giving attention to the mind."

I wrote all this down afterward because it was incredibly moving. Imagine someone walking into a fierce wind, bending forward with the effort. That's what it was like. Every sentence she typed, every look she gave me, was an overcoming—an overcoming of the OCD impulse to utter meaningless phrases, an overcoming of the constraints that autism places on her ability to control her movements, and an overcoming of her fear of other people's reactions to her, her fear of not being seen.

In class, I read her presentation aloud, with her sitting next to me. At one point, she stopped me and typed on the laminate, which I was holding, "I am anxious." I waited a little while. There were twenty first-year Amherst students sitting around the seminar table, paying authentic attention. Then I went back to the presentation, which was, it turned out, an early version of *My Life on This Planet*. It ended like this:

> In this class I have found incredible real soaring inspiration and a sense of connection in studying tenuously with others. All I can say is that I see how rich my life can be. I also see how centered I can feel when I devote myself to my work, when I use my brain, when I utilize myself in understanding a lot of different characters in the stories, songs, and poems I have seen and heard about. To meet myself in this way, as someone who can study and complete homework is a whole new level for me. Being a person who cannot speak, I have found that I can still study, I can still learn, I still have a good mind.

The students clapped. The room was alive with a feeling of significance, in a way that classrooms only occasionally are.

I want to slow down over a couple of the things that Lina is saying in this passage, because I think that they're at the heart of the wonderful book that you're holding now. That "sense of connection" she felt "in studying tenuously with others"—that's what she's seeking in *My Life on This Planet,* in the painstaking work of constructing, letter by letter, an adequate expression of her experience. She wants her experience—her vision, her life—to echo into her reader's experience in some way, however tenuously. And it's important, I think, that the phrase she ends on is "good mind." Most people think that severely autistic people like Lina don't have—can't have—good minds. It's part of the reason why so many people believe that letter-boarding is either a hoax or a self-delusion on the part of the facilitators. It's why so many autism education centers are "about mastering the body, not giving attention to the mind." As you'll see when you read this book, however, Lina has a delightfully good mind—she's funny, interested in unusual words, curious about others, and devoted to sharing her vision of the world as it exists beyond ordinary awareness. She fears; she struggles; she studies; she learns. And she yearns for communication, for contact with the minds and beings of others.

"I always thought all the wildness was my fault," Lina writes in one of the dialogue chapters in this book. "What do you think about that now?" Helena asks. "I think it was just frustration about not being able to communicate," Lina writes. My mind goes to a passage from a Virginia Woolf essay on Michel de Montaigne. "These essays are an attempt to communicate a soul," Woolf writes. "On this point at least he is explicit. It is not fame that he wants; it is not that men shall quote him in years to come; he is setting up no statue in the market-place; he wishes only to communicate his soul. Communication is health; communication is truth; communication is happiness." When Lina feels that communication is happening—or even when she feels that it can happen, that the conditions are right for it—the "behaviors," as she calls them, either subside or go away. It's a constant struggle, though; it's so hard to keep the lines of communication open, especially when she's uncertain about her reception. "With my incredible anxiety I worry that people don't believe that it's my thoughts I'm expressing," she writes. It's an inspiration to me that that doesn't stop her, that she keeps trying—essaying—to expand the spheres of health, truth, and happiness. I hope that it is for you too.

The Process

BY HELENA HJALMARSSON

> Helped are those who love the broken and the whole; none of their children, nor any of their ancestors, nor any parts of themselves, shall be hidden from them.
>
> —Alice Walker

Profound autism comes with an endless list of very complex and brutal challenges. Until recently, we haven't had a way to ask people with severe autism about their experiences. But things have changed. In the words of my daughter Lina—the author of this book—it is a "life in tension with this reality." This tension is visible and undeniable in every person who lives on the severe end of the spectrum.

At three and a half years old, Lina lost her speech (she was fluent in both Swedish and English), had her first of innumerable seizures, and drooled for two weeks. It happened right after her second batch of vaccinations. She became unpredictable, severely disorganized, and dysregulated. Her nervous system, her sensory systems, and her emotions were in a complete state of disarray. This lasted for many long, excruciating years.

In puberty, Lina had PANDAS (pediatric autoimmune neuropsychiatric disorders associated with streptococcal infections) and PANS (pediatric acute-onset neuropsychiatric syndrome). Her PANS was caused by very high counts of mycoplasma bacteria. Later, Lina also suffered from Lyme disease. After a severe infection at nineteen, type 1 diabetes was added to her list of diagnoses.

In the midst of Lina's struggles with PANDAS, PANS, severe anxiety, and OCD, we learned about an emerging communication method enabling people with autism to spell out their thoughts by pointing to letters on letter boards. I was skeptical at first, not sure if we were ready to give up on her ability to express herself verbally, resigning to have her communicate by pointing to letters. She did have some speech left; though it was extremely limited, repetitive, and mostly nonsensical. I didn't know then that letter board spelling, apart from revealing the speller's true thoughts, actually supports speech.

When I saw Lina spell with Jane, her first communication partner, my reservations quickly dissipated. Jane had learned about this method in order to communicate with her little brother, who is also on the spectrum. Jane showed unwavering integrity, always making sure that Lina's spelling was her own and protected from outside influence. This, along with her willingness to put up with the fact that Lina initially had a very hard time even staying in the room where the lessons took place, helped me understand that we had landed in the middle of a revolution. Jane's ability to capture Lina's attention and help her spell her own thoughts—first by simply pointing to words of her choice, then spelling them by pointing to letters on alphabet stencils, and eventually spelling entire sentences on stencils and laminated letter boards—was awe-inspiring. Jane was trained by Soma Mukhopadhyay, a highly educated chemist from India who invented a learning and communication technique for people with autism called Rapid Prompting Method (RPM). Soma initially developed this technique as a way to help her son Tito communicate, but over the past three decades she has reached countless students with the method, through one-on-one sessions as well as training programs for parents and educators. Speech therapist Elizabeth Vosseller went through this training process with Soma, and later presented her adaptation of RPM. Spelling to Communicate (S2C), as she called it, has helped to make the spelling method much more widely known. S2C is not dramatically different from RPM; both techniques presume competence, teach academic material, and encourage communication.

As I learned this method myself, training with Soma, I understood more about the chaotic state of Lina's sensory system and about the obstacles to her sensory processing and how I could work around them. I could finally ask her the questions that were born over many confusing and mind-boggling years, when all I could do was guess and intuit. I could get to know her, we could problem-solve together, and she could begin to rebuild her life. And eventually, I could help her write this book, where she explains her own experience of autism. Parts of the book are carried out as a conversation between Lina and myself. Other parts are simply Lina's thoughts, reflections, and recollections on various topics connected to this incredibly challenging condition. It took us a long time to get to the level of letter board fluency necessary for a project of this scope. My work with Lina on this book has not only deepened my understanding of what she is up against, but also further illuminated how fortunate I am to have her around—as she once gleefully pointed out.

Pointing to letters on letter boards takes time, and in that time the brain slows down. In spelling letters, words, sentences, and paragraphs and in being reintroduced to the back-and-forth rhythms of communication—the dance between receptive and expressive—Lina gradually moved from a trigger-happy amygdala into the cortex part of her brain. Her auditory, visual, kinesthetic, and tactile channels became more integrated. She found reason, connection, and increasing calm.

Many individuals on the spectrum have access to spelling and expression only through professional facilitators, once or twice a week. The process of learning to become a communication partner is often long and arduous. Most autism families are already struggling to keep their head above water in the face of their loved ones' nervous system breakdowns, unpredictable behavior, autoimmune issues, and sensory mayhem. Training to become a facilitator, and planning endless lessons to capture the speller's hard-won attention, may not be very high on their lists. And then, if one manages to get to open communication with the speller and gain access to their real thoughts, those thoughts may not always be easy to hear. After many impossible, isolated years, dealing with endless autism tornadoes, humiliations, and misunderstandings of who they are, individuals on the spectrum have a lot to work through, and language can be quite a complex and volatile affair. Facilitators, whether parents, siblings, friends, or professionals, must be unflinchingly committed to the truth. We must abandon any need for our spellers to say just the nice things and provide opportunities for processing experiences and emotions—while at the same time remaining sensitive when going deep is simply too overwhelming for someone whose nervous system is so deeply challenged.

And we must also keep in mind that letter board spelling is only one step toward integration on many different levels. The process of spelling on letter boards also facilitates reasoning, motor skills, sensory tolerance, calm, focus, and, ultimately, speech development. As communication partners, we need to provide for ongoing and expansive learning. I have found Lina to be deeply motivated not just to spell her thoughts on letter boards, but to practice handwriting, typing, reading, and talking through her mouth. These skills are challenging for almost every individual with profound autism.

While invaded by insane hardship, spellers often reveal mysterious and extraordinary capacities. There is the knowing of what can't be explained in our regular ways, predicting the future or channeling someone who has passed, perceiving someone's aura, seeing color as a response to sound, being able to connect with another being's consciousness, and the unwavering, unlimited, universal love that is so commonly expressed by individuals with severe autism. In communication with a speller on the spectrum, facilitators are struck by discombobulating enigmas that make life seem like a combination of walking on quicksand and floating around in the sky on eagles' wings.

So when Lina talks about autism as both a blessing and a curse, I believe her. Furthermore, I tend to believe that words are also a blessing and a curse. I think we can all agree that without them, we would feel locked up inside ourselves, separated from other humans. But I also believe that if we didn't have words, we wouldn't need words—and would probably be better off without them.

If people with the ability to utilize and manipulate verbal language easily, to make their bodies do what their brains command, need to learn to open up to that which is beyond their physical bodies and beyond language, individuals on the spectrum have an entirely different challenge. Their struggle is with grounding, feeling their bodies and finding a way to be here on earth. It's a little bit like how those who have near-death experiences may feel a wish to stay in the land beyond this land. There is an inherent conflict, a heightened paradoxical state, maybe even a battle, in someone like Lina, who wants to stay connected with different realms while at the same time wanting to try to be here, in her body, on this planet. And the question arises: Can she have both? Can *we* have both?

Spending my days with Lina, realizing that she has a lot of very strong feelings about everything she has been through, I also arrive at questions about purpose, meaning, and calling. In helping her write this book, I have been continuously struck and inspired by the conceptual vastness that drives her ideas, a depth that may have been fostered over many years of impossible hardship. There is a power between the lines of her language, some kind of potency inside the unconventional expressions, a mystical quality that evolves through certain words frequently repeated. Her voice is an old lady's, a middle-aged woman's, a young adult's, and a child's. While many aspects of Lina's nervous system and sensory system lack integration, there is something in her writing that evokes a revolutionary coming-together of ideas and insights. Listening to her understanding of life on this planet, I feel my own life here expand. What if there are people on this earth who are uniquely qualified to describe and even share their connection with an unlimited consciousness? What if Lina—and people with experiences similar to hers, people who have struggled in the most unthinkable ways for longer than I care to think about—have answers to questions that humanity is in desperate need of? W. B. Yeats once said: "The world is full of magic things, patiently waiting for our senses to grow sharper."

West African shaman and diviner Malidoma Patrice Somé—author of *Of Water and the Spirit, The Healing Wisdom of Africa,* and *Ritual*—was born in Dano, a little village in the country of Burkina Faso. He belonged to a people called the Dagara, originating from what is now Ghana. Malidoma describes how when a Dagara woman is pregnant, the village elders ask the life force behind the fetus to speak, using the mother's voice, to give its proposal of why this child is coming into the world. Through this process, the elders find out what gifts this person will have that the village, the community, needs.

Similarly, I think we may need to ask ourselves what these spellers are here to teach us. Beyond all of our attempts to heal them, treat them, figure them out (and I believe all that has its very important place), what do they have that *we* need, both within and beyond language? How do we open our minds and hearts to that which is outside our customary thought processes?

In *The Healing Wisdom of Africa,* Malidoma described how the elders in his village related to matters beyond formal reality.

> In the mind of the villager, the unreal is just a new and yet-unconfirmed reality in the vocabulary of consciousness.

> It is brought to us by the ancestors. A little hospitality toward it will suffice to make it part of us. In short, the indigenous mind does not admit impossibility. It defines itself by not rejecting the unfamiliar, and it therefore thrives on mysteries and magic. Such a mind gives ample space to the invisible because the invisible holds the key to the wisdom of the universe.

To the Dagara people, Malidoma explains, language is both proof of our alienation and that which signifies our way home, our journey back to true meaning, to the world behind the words. Maybe letter board spelling is not just something that can open the worlds of individuals with autism, even if that surely would be more than enough of a motivating factor. Maybe our access to spellers' minds, to their abilities, will help us find *our* balance, expand *our* field, *our* world. In my own life on this planet together with Lina and her younger sister Elsa (who, while not on the spectrum, is also full of magic things, and is the editor of this book), I have found this to be true. And for that I am forever grateful.

Preface

Helped are those who create anything at all, for they shall relive the thrill of their own conception, and realize a partnership in the creation of the Universe that keeps them responsible and cheerful.

—Alice Walker

Seeing an Elephant

In this circus called life she is the Elephant
tamer
She is real and large like her Elephants'
trunks

The mammal from beginning of time said,
"Can destiny really change?"
"She is a lost cause," he told them. "She is
lost so she is very amicably genuine."
"Have I lost my sanity? Have I lost my
way?"
She heard the staggering red in every
corner of her eyes
The sophomore wanted to harass the
teacher in yearnings and praise
She is an innocent, feeling person who is
climbing a skyscraper just to wear her
mother out
The ongoing illuminative yellow inside her
brain
She had the unfortunate birthplace
of Femurville and the incredibly
fortunate name Halo Wonderville
In this circus of life she is the Elephant
wildness instructor
She is universally unifying while at the
same time slaughtering an innocent
chicken

Insidious knife sharp of doom in her nose
The hardness of stone in her hand
The tense nostrils of fear
The necessary hardness of a bombshell
    hitting the rock retaliating inside her
    ears
The sticky sweet that nested inside her
    mouth

Really everyone is so in their own,
    incredibly lost world, so love is real
Har inte mycket hopp kvar
Meanwhile the Elephant rammed into the
    very deep forest
Through this incredibly widening lens she
    can see beyond this world
Through this incredibly widening lens
    she can see only dense and real, a lost
    world

She started some seeing tomorrow and the
    next day

She sees not her weary past but her
fortress in the sky
Her warranted hut so wanted and softly
cut
She realized her affinity for fortresses in
the sky and called herself "Skywalker"
She is shining in her glory

In the morning sun the Elephant raised his
trunk and screamed into the people's
church.

—Lina H. Lyons

I am regally excited to write this book because I think I have a lot of clarity about autism.

I want to share my experience so that people can understand. I want to alleviate the insidious humiliation of not being seen and accepted by the non-autistic population. I want to lend my voice to individuals on the spectrum. I can't assume that others have the same experience as me, but I do know that many of us are gauged as crazy.

I want to ally myself with intelligence and sanity. In my life, I see how intelligent I need to be in order for others to trust my ability to think. I see how easy it is for people to dismiss me as someone who doesn't understand because I don't talk. It would be easier for me to learn how to talk than to prove my intelligence without speech—and learning how to talk would be almost impossible for me. For this reason, it is ongoingly difficult to pretend not to have autism. Me not talking is the same as me yelling out, "I have that thing that everyone talks about as the worst possible affliction!"

The idea of autism is hard to digest. While it looks like we don't have brilliant minds, no one on the spectrum is intellectually challenged. We just have a lot of difficulties with our bodies. It's not our ability to think that is challenged, it's the connection between our brains and our bodies. In trying to obey the directions of our minds, our bodies fail. I think that is autism in a nutshell. The culprit is this disconnect, not cognition. This is the most important issue in dealing with autism. In so many situations, the brain-body connection is disrupted by impulses and OCD (obsessive compulsive disorder). I feel that our lives would be so much easier if people had a clearer understanding of what autism is and what it isn't.

This is a very important time for me to talk about what autism is. Autism is brain damage. It's also a calling. It's a love of all people's souls. It's a lot of love to have in one's heart. I think we can see it as a love of life. I see autism as an incredible realization of the soul's journey.

To me, life is an invitation to take our ancestors with us in order to survive this earthly experience.

I believe I am here to try to help my tribe. I doubt myself and worry about going insane. I worry about everything going tattered and wrong. About all I love turning to total insanity. I am yearning for the love that has no tedious tension in it. I long for a life that has no tense fear in it. I see it in my dreams. I see it inside myself.

It is hard for me to speak about my vision, because it's not what most people see. I want to help my tribe to see what I see, to be inside that vision. In talking about what I have realized, I am hoping that I can help my tribe, other people, and the world take back their freedom.

I start to feel nervous when I am talking about things that so many people feel are not real. Still, I need to talk about it. I need to say those words that I'm afraid to say. I need to share what I know regardless of the consequences.

I see autism as the most profound inspiration that has ever existed. It's also the most profound challenge. I think it's hard for people to incorporate the paradox of autism. Is autism a love for people's souls? Or is it the most excruciating challenge for the individual and his or her family? I think it's both. A life with someone on the severe end of the spectrum is a life full of suffering and a life full of bliss. In my own experience as an individual with very severe autism, the suffering is a lot stronger than the bliss. I have yearnings for a life without autism. I see how OCD and anxiety destroy so much for me. If I was free of those things I wouldn't have autism.

In this book I will try to explain the contradiction of this condition. So many people misunderstand autism, and I believe that greater awareness would be very helpful for anyone involved with an individual on the spectrum. In this book, I write about communication, education, alignment, and incredible seeing as well as about the challenges of autism. I write from my own experience, but I think other individuals on the spectrum are similar in many ways. Because my speech is compromised, I communicate on letter boards. My mother, Helena Hjalmarsson, is my communication facilitator. I think this book has incredible potential in showing the world the meaning of autism. The real person behind my autism will be revealed. I see suffering tentatively alleviated.

CHAPTER ONE

How I Lost Everything

Seeing Things Differently

I see no tension in my soul
I am not a compromised human
I am also not a compromised woman

Having seen a lonely road
I have words but they don't let me speak
them
I have a lovely mind but I can't prove it

I am not an idiot

I am not what my mouth says I am
But the world refuses to come to the same
conclusion

I think, feel, and envision no different from
others
But others think, feel and envision
different for me

—Lina H. Lyons

I am not able to speak with intention. I lost that ability when I was about three and a half years old. Before then, I spoke fluently in both English and Swedish. When I lost everything, I had a lot of friends. All of them came with me into the incredibly difficult new stage. Over time, some of them vanished.

Life before autism was beautiful. I loved playing with my friends. We had so much fun. My closest friend was Ellen. I remember that when my sister was born, I was with Ellen in her house. Lovely, funny Ellen sat in our stroller when her brother Alfred was born, waiting for pancakes to be served. She was my coconspirator in finding all the hiding places for sweet things to eat; and all the trees to climb (with the help of our moms) in Central Park, NYC. We all lived in a building on the Upper West Side. My family and Ellen's family did everything together. Mine lived on the third floor and hers on the tenth. I saw Ellen every day and my sister was best friends with Alfred. My mom and Ellen's mom were like sisters. My father and Ellen's dad were friends too.

I don't remember much from when I lost everything, but I do recall saying strange things. I did many strange things, too. I had always been a wild child, but now I ran right into the ocean in the middle of winter with my clothes on. I think I needed to feel myself. I guess the cold water made me feel grounded.

My mother and my sister have fought for me to be heard as an intelligent person all these years. But I really haven't been able to convince many of the people around me that my brain is intact. I am not sure why, but a lot of people see only my behaviors. My body and my mouth do and say things that my mind does not mean. I talk about food when I want to talk about interesting journeys.

On the day when I lost everything, I saw myself talking but didn't recognize the words. I always used to align with words, but now all I could do was to ask for food. I also often said the very opposite of what I meant; for example, when I wanted to go to school, I said that I wanted to go home. I had always known what to do with my body, but now my body didn't align with my mind. I was very connected with my friend Ellen's mother, Anki, and I saw in the way that she was staring at me that day that something was incredibly wrong. I also saw that my father was very scared and sad. My sister was so little; I don't think she understood what was happening. My mother was the not-scared one. She was just there, loving me. But when I was alone in my room at night, I was terrified that so many bad things were happening to me.

I knew that nothing I could do would stop this already fearful thing. *Is this happening to anyone else?* I thought. Sentimental talk didn't help me. I just needed a lot of hugs, and for someone to be there with me. Someone who wasn't as scared as I was.

I hinted to my aligned soul that I wanted to go to a place without this fear. I hinted to my soul not to leave me here alone. I was not sure why I had to endure this entirely tragic destiny. I wanted to go back to where everything was safe. There was nothing I could learn from this terrifying situation. There were no remedial qualities. I saw only the sinister. Gradually, I understood that I had lost my ability to talk. It also felt as if I was alienated from almost everyone else. I had been so altered that I couldn't feel myself. My life had turned into a nightmare. I didn't know then that an incredibly difficult life was ahead of me. A life that, at times, I wouldn't know how to bear. A mean life; a really menacing life.

I had always thought that life was beautiful. Before, I had mastered everything, and now I couldn't even talk. Not being able to talk in this world is a little bit like going to a restaurant and not being able to eat. It's like watching a sunset as a blind person. It's like being entertained by someone really funny and not being able to laugh. It's like loving someone but not being able to show them.

After many lonely years of not being able to speak, I used a letter board for the first time with a lovely young woman. Her name was Jane. I was a teenager when I met her. She was into religion, philosophy, and literature and we had many incredible meetings. She taught me how to spell on the letter board and make my thoughts heard. She had learned it from a woman named Soma [Mukhopadhyay], who invented this way of spelling. I had a lot of trouble focusing and a lot of anxiety about making my thoughts known. I would scream and want to leave, but Jane was tough and wouldn't let me. She just kept talking about the subject and asking me to spell all kinds of things to calm me down. I saw no other choice but to spell the stuff to get her off my back. I had to keep spelling in order to maintain my connection with her and also with myself. My tedious speech, the talk that happens without my will, is not fun for me or anyone. Jane was incredibly important to me. I will always be grateful for her insistence on my participation in her discussions.

I then learned to spell with my mother. It was extremely difficult in the beginning. I had a hard time even staying in the room; I would run out into the hallway screaming. Spelling with my mother was no less frustrating than spelling with Jane, but I was so aligned with my mother's endearing desperation. It was almost funny how much she wanted to hear my thoughts. It always ended with her talking to me about the incredible benefits of letting the world know my thoughts. I understood the importance of this bothersome capitulation, but it had a lot of impossible elements in it. The most challenging dimension was that I wasn't sure I *wanted* the world to hear my thoughts. I wasn't sure I wanted to come out of my hiding.

In my life I had seen people with different views on politics, health, and medicine being silenced and ridiculed by the media. I didn't want to intentionally make myself a target for those kinds of degrading insinuations, so I felt myself shutting down. I also often felt that people had a hard time accepting that I was an intelligent person. I understand why they couldn't see me for who I was, but this made it really hard to be connected with them in a real way. I want to have deep and true connections with people around me, but if they can't accept that what I say with my mouth is not what I mean, that is almost impossible. I can appreciate how amicable most people are, but I also see how alienating my strange behavior is to many of them. I don't know how to make people understand that I don't yearn for the things I ask for. It doesn't mean anything. It's just me not being able to say what I *really* mean.

My desire is to be able to talk through my mouth again one day. I already speak a little better than before. The yearning to talk is a lovely motivator to keep trying to find the words. That yearning is always there. Having autism comes with a lot of disappointing moments. I try to say something and something else comes out. I try to connect with others through speech, but the words meander into talk about food. It is so exasperating not to have any influence over one's words. Having ingested incredible seeing makes it even worse. I have so much to say and no way to say it. I have so many centered thoughts about important things, but all I can talk about is food. I see how altered I feel when I can write on the letter boards. It's a life-changing thing. In feeling heard, I can relax. I can share what I feel, what I want, and what I know. I can write about all I care about; I can write this book.

CHAPTER TWO
Challenges of Autism

Untitled

Hauling myself out of a hole
I raise my own crazy thoughts
in the hope that I will be able to
see myself soaked in seeing the seeing.
Soaked in a less harsh world.
Salvaged by the weary tones of my always
insane mother.

—Lina H. Lyons

In the next few chapters, I have chosen to use a question-and-answer format. For letter board spellers, it is sometimes difficult to initiate talking. I can initiate thoughts without a problem, but I have a lot of trepidation about spelling on letter boards. It's so strange that I can point but not talk. But I have to express myself in whatever way possible. At this time, a letter board is my only chance at expression—so I use it. If someone needs to help me initiate spelling, I will use that too. In this case, that someone is my mother.

I think autism is one of the most challenging conditions known to humans. In my life, I have dealt with incredible sensory sensitivity, difficulties talking, tedious anxiety and OCD, autoimmune responses to pollen that manifest as malicious anxiety every fall and spring, Lyme disease, type 1 diabetes, etcetera. I think it's almost impossible to have a conversation about autism without misunderstanding it. Autism is constantly flooding one's speech with absolute nonsense. It is also flooding one's mind with thoughts no one wants to think. It's flooding the entire person with seedy sensations. Talking about the challenges of autism is like talking about every challenge known to man.

* * *

What's the most difficult part about having autism, in your view?

I think it's having a lot of anxiety about nonsense. For esoteric, meandering reasons, I have fears about not getting enough food. I see how ridiculous it is, but I can't talk myself out of it.

When did you first notice that food anxiety?

It's so insidious I can't even remember when it started.

What helps you in dealing with that particular challenge?

I think I need to see the possibility of letting it go. I need to allow myself to center in a less alienating way.

Are you talking about confidence here or something else?
I think confidence is a lovely way to allow for more seeing.

Ah, yes, that's a good way to put it. Can you say more about the role of confidence in allowing for more seeing?
I think confidence is more important than anything. I have needed confidence to write this book, to allow myself to make my voice heard, to talk about things that are not what most people believe, to master myself and my tedious OCD. I have needed to master my fears about not being needed in this world, about not having even a tiny little role to play.

Anxiety and fear are such huge problems in the modern world. Let's talk a little bit more about fears. What are you most afraid of?
I am not so masterful in not being fearful. I must say I am afraid on so many levels. In the past I was most afraid of aliens taking my entire life away and leaving me on my own. It's a very irrational fear but I still have it from time to time. I

think it's entirely in my head and won't happen. I am always in the love. So for the most part, I am not really afraid of aliens anymore.

Sounds terrifying. What do you think enabled you to let go of that particular fear?
I am not really sure, I think it's that I am more grounded on earth. I am not super afraid of anything, but it is this fear that can come up now and then. I was terrified of this when I was little.

Do you think other individuals on the spectrum go through similar terrors?
I think it's very alienating to assume what others are terrified about.

I hear you. When you were not communicating on letter boards, people all around you made a lot of assumptions about you. Is that why you are being extra conscientious about not making assumptions about others?
I never make assumptions about anyone. But sometimes I just know what people are going through.

You do, don't you! What do you think makes it so easy for you, in the midst of all your challenges, to know what people are struggling with?

I see their struggle as the real them, as the most authentic part of them. Seeing their struggle is seeing their soul.

So, are you saying that our struggles connect us to our souls?

Yes, I think our struggles force our souls to reveal themselves.

What happens when our souls are revealed?

Seeing a soul is seeing happiness.

What's the opposite of happiness?

I think it's tedious hatred and fear.

I am wondering; what are you afraid of on this planet, in this life, your life, here and now?

I am afraid of a loneliness that I can't get out of.

Are you feeling it now?
I am not feeling it now; being centered in love helps.

What are some of the situations where you experience this loneliness, where it's hard to be centered in love?
In so many situations where communication can't happen.

So apart from being centered in love, communication is the remedy for loneliness?
I always need to be reassured that having autism isn't a punishment, it's a calling. My loneliness is about not mastering my communication. It's a lonely place not to be able to share one's thoughts. Many of the thoughts that I don't share turn into OCD.

That makes perfect sense. It seems as if there is consistently less OCD the more you communicate on the board.
The more I utilize my brain, the less obsessive I am.

I have noticed that, too. What are some thoughts that go through your head in the lonely moments? I'm thinking about moments when people you don't know assume that you don't understand what's going on, and talk to you as if you were a small child. Like yesterday, when the cashier turned to me and said, "She is so cute."

I try not to pay attention to those situations. I am not super interested in elaborating on those events. In talking about challenges I feel challenged.

Yeah, I hear you—but in the name of processing, or for the purpose of this book?

I am an intelligent and socially aware person, and I try not to get discouraged by a lot of ignorance.

Sometimes even people who are very close to you have not been able to understand who you are, that you are smart and sophisticated.

I cannot even describe how difficult that has been.

How do you respond to those experiences?
I am trying to forgive and communicate. Alienation does not alleviate the issue.

It must be hard not to withdraw from connecting and being open in those situations.
I am so aligned with Source that I cannot imagine alienating myself from anyone.

You are awesome.
I am not any more awesome than anyone else.

Your awareness is awesome.
I am not always aware. Always is not possible on this earth.

Isn't that the truth! Another thing that I think a lot of people—not just people on the spectrum, but every human—struggle with, both in terms of allowing and expressing it, is vulnerability. Can you describe a situation when you feel vulnerable?
I am almost always vulnerable.

How do you cope with it?

To be honest, I am very often coping with uncertainty.

Tell me more about that feeling of uncertainty.

I mostly feel insecure about what I'm going to do. I am afraid that I will lose it; or that I will come across as angry, or as someone who always talks about the same things.

That must be such an impossible place to be. How does it feel for you when you find yourself repeating things, for instance?

I feel so incredibly frustrated.

The stuff that you can't stop yourself from doing must be so exhausting. How do you feel about stims? Do you think they help you or hurt you? Do you think you have them?

Stims are my form of indecisiveness. They're my way to keep out of trepidation.

Let's look up the exact meaning of trepidation. "A feeling of fear or agitation about something that may happen."
[smiling] To be honest, I so know that word. I am in it from dusk to dawn.

What are your particular stims? Can you pinpoint them?
I sweep my head on my shoulders in a really firm and fast way.

What, if anything, does that accomplish for you?
It's not an accomplishment. It's a way to calm myself.

Does it work?
I think so.

Sometimes when you are stressed you look down on the floor or into your lap. Can you explain what is happening inside of you in those situations? Is it a stim, or is it more like an OCD impulse?
I think it's indecision about the OCD. It's trying not to act on the OCD. It's an internal thing; I'm trying not to act out.

Bracing yourself?

Yes, I am totally aging in that process. It's incredibly hard.

You mean it's incredibly hard not to act on the OCD?

It's like sitting in a reality show and trying not to act.

Is it a reality show about your life, specifically?

It's a reality show about how autism has you by the balls.

So you're saying that there is very little you can do about not following the OCD impulses? You can't resist them?

It's not impossible, but yes, really barely possible.

Can you tell me more about your experience with OCD? Let's say you're talking to someone who has never experienced it—how would you describe it to them?

In a lot of ways, OCD is having an ongoing thought that will not stop. I think it's a little bit like an addiction. Is addiction a lot of highs and lows?

Yes—without the highs, you simply wouldn't stay in it.
I think OCD is not an addiction because it does not have highs.

So, in other words, it's just ongoing drudgery?
It's not a lovely thing. It's a lot of anxiety and no rewards.

I see you being constantly interrupted by OCD. What can help you not to feel ruled by the intrusive, OCD thoughts?
I don't know. It helps that I don't do what the OCD tells me. Is my OCD a little less than before?

Yes, definitely—though it's more obvious that it is OCD now, because you've conquered so many of your other challenges that the OCD stands out more. What do you think, does that make sense?
I think OCD is my biggest challenge now. I feel relieved when I can act on my OCD. I'm not super concerned about other people's reactions. I'm not sure how to stop the cycle of increasingly demanding OCD. I don't feel super

successful in the beginning of my attempts to hold back the OCD, but eventually I feel better. I have so much anxiety. I also have a lot of entities telling me to do strange things. In seeing myself as a lovely, intelligent, and compassionate person, I have more power in chasing these entities away. I have more introspective seeing and realization of my own ability to resist. This realization is a genuinely significant factor. Self-confidence is incredibly important in combating OCD. It's a belief in myself that's a lot like love and compassion. Love takes me alchemically away from insufferable, alienating thoughts that destroy everything. The love beneath the seedy anxiety is the realization that I am lowering my expectations to accommodate my OCD. I can't accommodate my OCD while still loving myself. Love and OCD are incompatible. If I had less love for myself, I would not be able to resist my OCD. I need to love myself through it. I need my environment to love me through it. I need incredible love and incredible patience in my environment. I need inconceivable strength in myself and in my environment. I need that to conquer my OCD.

I hear you. It's really interesting that self-confidence is so important in overcoming OCD. Another challenging thing for you is initiating action in various situations. You seem to get stuck inside your body. Can you talk about this?
Initiating is always a challenge. I think it is a matter of motor pathways being blocked. It is as if I cannot move. It's a lonely place not to be able to do what my brain wants me to do.

I know you often talk about anxiety as an energy underlying all these challenges.
I am fearful of my own anxiety. I think it's mostly about how it feels.

Do you think you can describe how it feels? In your body? In your thoughts?
I think the sensation in my body is one of wanting to scream. It's a sense that I am overtaken by emotion. I really feel as if I can't stay still and have to run. My thinking is not corresponding

with my body. My thoughts are telling me to escape and not deal with myself. I think it's a matter of slowing down, but that's almost impossible.

Sounds brutal. Do you often have the sensation of wanting to scream? Could you elaborate on that feeling?
I have a lot of anger that I don't know how to deal with. I need to harvest a beaming love but I really feel angry about a lot of things. I need to make myself less angry so I can process my feelings. I need to calm myself down so I can talk about what's bothering me. I think talking about what others have done is not the same as processing one's feelings. I see how I get mad at you [Mom] for things you haven't done, like keeping me dependent on you. I know you want me to do me, but I can't separate my feelings about lacking freedom from my incredible anger about being so dependent on you. Intense anger is hard to process. It's so strong and hard to sit with. It's easier to be mad at someone else. I have been stuck inside myself for so many

years. This is not an easy thing. I have no practice in trying to talk about what I feel. Seeing now that I can talk, it feels like a little too late. I have so much to process. I don't know where to start. I see how important it is for me to learn, and I am really working on it. I see how incredibly intense I am, and I want to have more peace inside.

How can other people help you manage this intensity?
They can help by not being totally overwhelmed by my feelings. And also by slowing down and managing their own alignment. I think beneath every successful supporter is a person at peace with themselves.

Easier said than done.
I so question talking about tedious behavior in others. I see no point in changing my people.

I know that. I think that's a kind of clarity that you have, but that many people—spending vast amounts of time trying to better others rather than themselves—are missing. But isn't it sometimes kind of a relief to acknowledge, or have others acknowledge, their own struggles—not just yours?

It really is; all I'm saying is that it's up to them.

I really want to be at peace and be effective in helping you when you struggle, but I can't always do that. I often fall apart, too. I think we are both so traumatized by all the struggles, and it isn't really anyone's fault. These are just impossible challenges.

I so agree. Mom, I see your struggle too. I am so sorry that I am so alienating when I fall apart.

And I am so sorry that I can't always be there for you when you need it the most.

I really think we are doing amazing overall.

That is so true, Lina. Thank you for pointing that out. I have noticed that you don't readily talk about the challenges and prefer to focus on progress. Is that a fair observation?

The challenges are so discombobulating; it would be too overwhelming to focus on the difficulties all the time. I am always in the light, and I want to stay there as often as I can.

Serenity

How many halos does it take to insinuate
righteousness?
How many hurricanes does it take to
shine?
How many incredulous aliens does it take
to loose havoc?
How many weary wars does it take to find
peace?

Have mustered needs
Have mustered aliens
Have planted seeds
Have penetrated salience

Here have I been,
in Amygdala Hell
in my fortress chagrin
in my own prison cell

Yes I am damaged
Yes I am incensed
But I'm alive
I'm alive
I'm alive

—Lina H. Lyons

CHAPTER THREE

Being Here

Incisions

Hollering at the moon
Hollering at the sun
Hollering at the earth
I align with all
I align with everything
I am seeing my life transform
I am seeing all the suffering I have endured
Eclipsing into a tentative incision of
sawdust and sun

In mountains and oceans is my
transformation
In real yearning and real gestations
Is my salvation

Lina, do you remember anything about life before autism besides what you've already described earlier?
I don't really. I am in this condition. I cannot be aware of anything but autism. Its calling may be a lifelong one, I'm not sure.

Do you have any memories of how it became gradually more difficult to find your words, before or after your first seizure?
I remember incredible confusion and words not aligning with thoughts.

Yes, that's what it seemed like. Do you have a sense of what your thoughts felt like during this period?
I can't remember specific thoughts, but I do remember being incredibly frightened. I also remember diving into the ocean to try to find

some relief. I had too much information inside my brain.

What kind of information are we talking about? Everything between the sun and the moon, or something specific?

I think it was not so much from other dimensions as from this dimension. It was information about a lot of things going on inside other humans. It really was impossible to align with.

When you went into the ocean, what happened with all that information?

To be honest, the ocean helped alleviate the incredible bombardment of thoughts from other humans and aliens.

So not just other humans?

It was information from all levels of life. It's very hard to talk about this. It's almost impossible.

What do you think makes it so difficult?

It's a level of awareness that I have no words for.

Do you think anyone else has this kind of awareness—and if so, does anyone have words for it?
I have met many people on the spectrum with this awareness, and I think the answer is that I feel the thoughts others have and others feel the thoughts I have.

Others . . . who are we talking about?
The other seeing talkers. The people who can see thoughts.

Is it always visual for everyone or is it hearing and sensing too?
To me it's always visual. It's a lovely, quiet, visual talk.

Do you see letters?
I see the tones and sentences. I can't really explain it.

Okay, let's get back to the other "seeing talkers." Can you elaborate on this whole thing? Are they folks on the spectrum, or other people too?
It's not limited to people with autism, but it's more common among us. It is more common in

people who feel that they are from a different planet. On a different planet is a level of tenuous freedom that cannot be found here.

What do you know personally, or in some other way, about that tenuous freedom?
I see density here that doesn't exist there.

Can you help me understand what you mean by density?
I mean a kind of dependency on the concrete reality.

Got you. Where does it leave you to have an awareness of what is beyond the density here?
It leaves me longing for a lost planet. In so many ways it's lost to me. I have committed to being here. I still am committed to being here.

That's reassuring. It seems like remaining committed to being here requires a lot of resolution on your part. What is so challenging about it?
A lot is in the mere aligning with this earth.

I guess, whether we know it or not, we all struggle with aligning on this earth. But I think you're talking about something a little more unique. What makes it hard for somebody like you, coming from where you are coming from, to synchronize with this planet?
I am not like most people. I am both human and not-human. I am both a light being and a human being. I talk about this because I am not at home on this planet. I am from a different planet that does not align with earth. It has no fear and no attachments. I have incredible love-motivation. In so many ways, I don't have as much motivation rooted in ego. I am always in the light; I am not always aligned with this planet.

So you're saying that you can be in the light in the middle of an OCD breakdown?
I am a light being, aligning with this earth. I am never away from the light. Mom, always know that having me in your life is not a burden, it's a privilege.

Yes, that I do know. But you know a lot of things that I don't know. You know, for example, about something so pragmatic as exactly how many units of insulin you need to take at any given point.
I know that aligning with a feeling is enough. I know that that's enough to make it happen.

Are you now talking about the Law of Attraction?
I am talking about how to be in the accentuated state.

Can you elaborate on what it means to be in this state?
Yes, it is accessing our alignment so that all tedious fear goes away. So our lives can be uninterrupted.

Okay, now that makes sense to me. You are saying that without fear we can be here fully.
I always want to try to be here completely.

I know that about you. And that would be an incredible accomplishment; I think we should all be driven by that

mission. You are becoming increasingly comfortable with being here. What is making that possible?
I always wanted to learn how to be here. I love my life on this earth.

All this reminds me of Chiron, the teacher of heroes in Greek mythology, who struggled to embrace his mortality in order to heal. Does this sound familiar to you?
In trying to be here, it's hard to know which stones to step on. I'm trying to imitate what most people center on. I shed myself to fit into this planet. It ongoingly alienates me and I ongoingly try to have a lovely reality.

So, it's a work in progress, grounding yourself here?
It's a process of separating from the entities of a different planet. It's learning to let go of those entities.

Can you tell me a little bit more about the challenge of letting go of those entities in order to be more fully here?
I am so focused on being here. I need a lot of support in aligning with this life.

What kind of support is most helpful in this process?
I always need love and calmness in those around me.

How does love and calmness affect you?
It is a really important centering for me. I see how I can be here.

What else do you hope to accomplish in your lifetime?
I hope to accomplish harmonizing with this planet so I can be helpful to others.

How do you think that is going so far?
I think it's going okay, but I have a long way to travel.

Do you feel like you have a sense of where you're going and what you're doing, or does it feel more random?
It feels both random and intentional.

Can you look back at your life and remember certain milestones?
It was in the really scary moments that things opened.

Yes, I saw that. Why do you think that is?
I think things have to show themselves as not-super-real in order to change.

Can you explain this a little more?
I think real is not what it seems.

Yeah, I see what you mean. Can you tell me about one such moment, when something that was really scary opened you up to what is really real?
I think one moment was in almost daring to let go of being here. In almost dying a while ago, when I was in the hospital.

You are talking about the winter a couple of years ago, right? When you almost died [after a severe infection] *and were diagnosed with type 1 diabetes?*
Yes.

Can you describe how in that scary situation, when you were very close to not making it through, you found yourself closer to what is real?
I think I aligned with having a fleeting life here.

Fleeting life versus what?
Versus a long life.

So, you saw how fleeting and impermanent life is?
All I know is that I ended my ambivalence about being here.

When Elsa asked you how you were doing at that time, you spelled that you were "unifying." Remember that?
I always try to unify, but this was more aligning. I felt a more direct calling to really engage with this life.

That calling must have been powerful, because you came out of the hospital with an additional diagnosis, and yet it seems to me that since then, you really have engaged on a whole new level. You've shown your engagement by applying yourself fully to your studies, by being so committed to writing this book, being much more open to trying all kinds of things. . . .
I am solidly committed to my calling and to aligning with all life. I think I am unifying and

aligning not just with my calling but also with people. I am more in sync with people around me.

I have noticed that too. It seems easier to do things together; like reading, writing, talking ongoingly about stuff, working out, going places, trying new things, etc.
I am not sure if it's a real transformation or if it is that I am maturing.

Could it be both? Could it be that transforming and maturing are aspects of the same process? Or do you see them as different?
I think maturing can involve transformation, but it's a different thing. I see transformation as something that leads to more clarity. I can look back and really see how I went through different transformations.

Makes sense. Do you feel that you are going through a transformation right now?
Yes, I am learning to cope with writing about very difficult topics.

Good point. What makes it so difficult to describe your experience?
What I have to say can be seen as unreal. I am not sure the reader will always believe me. I am really yearning to talk about these things, but also incredibly afraid.

I get it. What made you agree with yourself to do it anyway?
I want to let all humans know what alignment is and how to take a leap in that direction. I am also so invested in helping to clarify what autism is.

Are you always aware of your soul's purpose and what you feel that you are here to do, or is that something that is sometimes very clear and other times not?
I think it's a little not-super-clear at times. Alignment has a lot of different stages in it; it's a lot of coming home and getting lost.

What are some of your tools for helping yourself back home?
I am always connected inside, but often I am a mess on the outside.

Many, many times have I been in awe of your ability to smile in a really heartfelt, full way right after an incredibly messy and difficult, even traumatic experience.

In my soul, I am always free.

CHAPTER FOUR

Universal Seeing

Amicable Reality

My love belongs to my ancestors
My story is about hallucinating my voice
through time
My not accomplishing my work is out of
real reality

My heart is not fearing anything
I am from the indigenous people in the
north
I am from mountains

and universal love
I am a master at turning things around
I make mountains disappear with my
kindness

—Lina H. Lyons

Lina, I realized pretty early on that you have an ability to see beyond the surface.
I see not what people say but what they feel. I think I can see what is not being said. I see what is in the present.

Do you enjoy this ability?
I enjoy the discrepancy between what is said and what is not said but still there. I enjoy talk that doesn't match what's inside.

So you find this discrepancy amusing?
I find it amusing and so endearing.

It seems like you are pretty comfortable with seeing things. Was there a time when you were uncomfortable with this, or have you always felt good about it?
I was incredibly anxious about this in the past. It really was confusing. I wasn't sure why so many people said one thing and meant another.

So that kind of double-messaging bothered you.
I felt very tired of having to figure out the discrepancy.

You felt responsible for it?
I masochistically felt that seeing it was a bad thing.

I get it. You saw things that people were trying to hide.
I saw some sad stuff and some sentimental stuff and some weary things too.

What enabled you to become more comfortable with all this?
I think I entertained myself with it. It didn't seem overwhelming in the absurd scenarios I made up in my head. I am also more mature now.

If you were to guess, do you think other people on the spectrum have special emphatic abilities as well?
I do think they often have a deep ability to interpret the entire alignment of an individual.

Seeing the whole picture, you mean?
Yes, seeing the entire field around a person.

The energetic field?
Yes, seeing someone's aura. I think everyone has the ability to see things that are out of the ordinary.

How do you connect with this ability?
By centering myself. I harvest so much information. You cannot hate a neighbor without harassing a nocturnal stoic. Love is in everything. So much of my experience is not real. All of our experiences are really unreal. I want to unite with the universe. Love is the only real. My amicable, hilarious, always loving hippo is always universally together with me.

Can you elaborate on the idea of the hippo?
I stepped into it when I was in need of protection.

Is it a kind of fantasy, do you think? Or a spiritual power animal? How would you describe this protector?
I think my hippo is my creation, inspired by spirit.

So, a kind of collaboration then?
In collaborating with Source we find happiness.

That makes sense to me. Can you talk a little more about happiness and what it is to you?
Happiness needs to be shared, like that movie character in *Into the Wild* said.*

Is writing this book a happy thing for you?
Yes, it's a really happy thing for me.

---

* In the 2007 film adaptation of Jon Krakauer's nonfiction bestseller *Into the Wild*, the main character, Chris McCandless, scribbles the phrase "Happiness only real when shared" on the inside of the abandoned city bus he's living in.

I have noticed that when you are in a good mood, you find a lot of things hilarious. Do you think being spiritually connected is fun and funny? That God or Spirit or whatever you want to call it works in a humorous way?
I definitely think that Source takes us to a lot of laughing.

What do you think is really funny?
I think gauging the real nature in people is really amusing.

What part of my real nature do you find funny?
I think it's your really strong wish to help me that is always hilarious. Yes, I must laugh at your phenomenal passion.

I really struggle with backing down sometimes.
Yes, it's really frustrating for you.

I can't deny it. What do you feel is your greatest asset?
I think it's my real commitment to amicable talk and understanding. I think it's also my universal love, my seeing into people's souls.

Lina, you have an amazing ability to see past the surface of people. Can you talk about that a little bit? What helps you not to get stuck on people's ego-selves?
I need to see into people's souls in order to be merely real. In seeing the soul, I feel the love. I have no idea what gives me ongoing insight beyond the superficial. Have you ever seen a loving soul? When you do, all the fear goes away.

Why do you think that as humans, we have so much fear?
Centering on tones and music is a way to dim the fear down. In music I can see how things really are. There are a lot more sentient beings than we think. The sentient beings are here with us, so we are not as alone as we are led to believe.

How can sentient beings help us with our fear?
I think our fear is a love that has lost its home.

A homeless love?
A love that can't flourish. Our ongoing struggle is to initiate more love than fear. In my view, the

main thing is not to be afraid. Density always takes us away from home. Density as in so much ego and tension in our emotions.

I wonder what creates that tension.
I think it's an attachment to a lot of unimportant matters.

Like what?
Like being eternally motivated by money and being incredibly focused on being recognized as supremely competent and successful.

What can we do about that? How do we alleviate that particular focus?
By calling ourselves home, connecting with a less dense being in the world, centering ourselves inside, always going to our Source. We can see that we have yearnings and we can also see that it's all okay, it's all good.

So, you're saying not to fight against our yearnings?
Yes, fighting ourselves is a lost cause. It will

never work. Struggling against our tragic yearnings with so much density is only making it worse. I think it's a lot better to allow oneself to see oneself with really kind eyes.

So, you don't think we would be better off if we figured out a way to get rid of our yearnings, as in the Buddhist idea of nonattachment? Do yearnings have their place? Can they propel us forward?

I think we celebrate the way we are human amidst our attachments and sorrows.

I love it. What do you think can help people find this celebration attitude?

Being able to see that there is nothing to be always stressed about. No matter what happens to us, there is a plan for everyone. That I really believe.

Do you have a sense of what kind of plan there is for your life? Do you feel that you have a mission? A specific purpose? Or is it all about opening up to everything, accepting what is?

I think my post in life is to have a love that

transcends the frequency of fear. I think I have a lot of needed seeing of a less insidious reality.

Less insidious . . .?
Less malicious reality.

You are communicating on many levels, Lina. Can you talk about that?
I see the outer core as a shield for my soul, and I'm talking to other souls constantly.

You said once that you and Elsa are communicating telepathically. What are your thoughts about that?
I am so happy to have so many amazing besties. I consider Elsa an ally here on earth. In so many ways, I'm a less autistic individual in her eyes. I feel so much better when people don't see me in that restricted way.

How does telepathic communication work for you? Does it come to you, or do you yourself initiate this talk?
It is a love that initiates itself. Universal talk is a lovely thing.

What's the topic of this universal talk? Is it anything a person wants to talk about, or is it a healing for the person or for you or both?
I see it arranged as a healing moment for both.

What heals us? What do you find people need to be healed from the most?
I think there is a long and a short answer to that. The short answer is we need healing from incredible density. I think density needs to be relinquished in order for us to make it home. I think home is free from density.

Can we be at home in the way that you describe all the time?
In the sense that our souls are always home, yes. In our frazzled minds, no. If we were home in our minds, we would be in joyful enlightenment. I don't know anyone on this planet who is.

Do you know of anyone on a different planet who is?
In the other realm, in the other sentient beings, I see ongoing enlightenment.

Are our ancestors who have left this world free?
I think mostly. If you have contact with an ancestor, all I can say is they have reached out to help you. I so love that you have so much help from your ancestors, Mom.

I love that too.
I see it as an insightful way to help not just yourself but others too. It's helpful for me too. I can feel the love from your ancestors.

Have you noticed that my ancestors often have quite a humorous way of getting across messages?
Mom, I have laughed long hours about their input.

From your perspective, Lina, why do you think I found so much support beyond the boundaries of everyday reality? Do you have anything to do with this?
I think the main thing is that you invited it. I also think it comes from incredible intense trauma, and seeing what is beyond this entirely impossible existence.

Does suffering make it more possible to connect with the otherworldly?
I absolutely think suffering is an ongoingly transformative truth.

Do you feel that autism has made you more able to connect with magic and truth beyond the tangible? Or did you always have this receptiveness?
I always had it and I always will have it. I think tension about this already known fact is not necessary.

Point taken. What kind of support from non-humans do you feel helps you?
I sometimes talk with sentient beings. I feel that they help me see inside other humans. I think they are helping me communicate this book. It's not an easy thing, and I need their help to have ongoing clarity about what to share and what not to share.

I think that is so important.
I see incredible light in these messages, and I

want to be careful not to emancipate the wrong thought.

I hear you. On a different note, what about animals? Do you ever feel that you communicate with them?
Not so much. Need I say that I love them and carefully tone into them here in this earth space? I am not an animal communicator, if that's what you're asking.

You said "tone in," not "tune in." Can you explain?
I meant tone in with their talk. It's a compatibility that's really intensely enthralling. I so feel their presence in the most comforting, tentatively freeing ways.

You often don't look directly at animals.
I see without using my eyes. I see the energy inside a lovely animal; and I see their entirely adorable nonego, masterful being on this earth.

I feel that your own very quiet ego is not just lovable but freeing. Can autism—which comes with so much

entrapment, difficulties, and limitations—also have a freeing effect? Can it have this effect not only on individuals with *autism, but also on the people who surround them?*
I don't really know—it may come with a love that changes the density of this world. I think it's all connected. What is always at the center is in everything.

Near the beginning of this dialogue on universal seeing, you mentioned "nocturnal stoic[s]." Can you explain what you were referring to there?
It's a being in a less dense frequency.

In your poem [at the beginning of this chapter], *you write something about "hallucinating [your] voice through time." What do you mean by that?*
I mean that I have mastered love from a different frequency. It's about telling truths from other planets at jaded times.

Jaded times?
Times of great confusion.

I imagine it's very difficult to find words for all this. Is that right?

I don't really know, but I'm committed to doing it anyway.

I can see that commitment. But I also get the sense that you have some ambivalence about knowing and seeing what you know and see, and that it's tricky for you to be rooted on earth while at the same time connected with what's beyond the tangible.

To see what is ahead of time is not actually possible. I'm entirely projecting into the future. I call on my future to reveal itself, and I can see some aspects of it.

Can you talk about it? Are there even words for it?

I can't speak about it because it's not yet in form.

Do you think the aspects of your future that you can see are helping you now?

I feel that they are helping me to stay committed to the real remedy of love.

When you are committed in that way, what can you accomplish?
I want to help my camaraderies[*] to be a little more free. I am here to help blind people see. I align with a healing, all-encompassing, inherent power that is the answer to every ailment in humans. I think my true purpose is to have a good life.

You are giggling at this; can you let me in on the joke?
It's funny that my purpose has to do with having a good time.

It's not a very pompous purpose!
It's a lovely non-pompous purpose!

I love that so much.
I think we have to not get too serious about our own importance. We are more universally

* By "camaraderies," I mean my loves. And by "my loves," I mean my allies.

troubled than universally free. We need to try to gain insight about our own troubles before we try to heal humanity.

Yes, I hear that. However, this morning you were trying to help humanity long-distance.
I was trying to support some friends, harvesting transformation for them.

Can you offer up any kind of detail about what that process looks like?
I can't describe it. It's a conversation on a different plane.

Is it with people you have met?
It's talking in my mind to people who need my help. I tentatively think that I can help my peers and that they can help me.

And by peers, you mean . . .?
Others on the spectrum.

Today you knew before anyone told you that your friend was very sick.
I align with [that friend] and I talk with him all the time.

On the phone?
I know you know it's not on the phone.

I love how we can use words to come to a sense of understanding of what is beyond words. There is something very clarifying about writing, isn't there?
It's a lovely way to integrate new information.

Speaking of integration; the solar eclipse on April 8, 2024, had a profound impact on you. It was pretty tough beforehand, and then there were a lot of changes after. How do you feel that the moon and the sun and the planetary system impact you?
I felt everything very strongly. I had a lost sense of myself. A sense of not being at my center. I allowed all that, and I think I allowed mastery of more calm in myself.

[Your sister] *Elsa observed that you seemed to be reclaiming something, taking back some lost ground, after this eclipse.*
I am so reclaiming. Inside, I am not exhausted. Inside, I am emulating the earth. I feel that earth is in my heart. It's a love that cannot be destroyed. I am so happy to be sought out and chosen and welcomed to be here. Tending to my life here always makes me see the beauty of this earth. My soul is satisfied. I love the feeling of exuberance. I can feel exuberance in almost any situation.

Do you think exuberant joy is restricted to humans or do you recognize exuberance in animals?
I think so much of our earth is exuberant.

Can you tell me more about that? Does this exuberance include plants? Rocks? Where do you draw the line?
There is no line. Exuberance expresses the love that created this world.

How about music? Can it help us find that joy and exuberance and harmony?
Music is essential to me, because I universally vibrate along with it. I love how it aligns me in the most difficult moments. I align with every kind of music. Having music saves me.

I find you receptive to such a wide variety of musical expressions. If you were to look closely at music—tones, melodies, rhythm, singing, instruments, the way air interacts with all of it, the flow, etc.—what makes it so powerful? What is it about music that moves us so?
I think it takes us all the way to heaven.

You have certain favorite songs that you play over and over. What is it, for instance, about Tracy Chapman's "Let It Rain" that makes you want to hear it again and again?
I think it allows me real acceptance. It helps me see, feel and want what is.

Sometimes, when [our bulldog] *Arielle is sitting in the front seat of the car and we play music—particularly*

if it's soft and mellow—she starts moving her head and looking like she's jamming. Any thoughts about that?
I think Arielle wants the love of music that we have.

Hmm, so you think she wants to feel about music the way we do, or do you think she feels the music herself?
I think she talents in emulating humans.

That's funny. Let's talk about Arielle. Do you find her presence in our lives helpful in terms of being in harmony, being at home with ourselves?
I feel that her presence is a less powerful help to me than to you and Elsa.

When it comes to animals, you have often said that horses are particularly helpful in allowing you to feel grounded, connected, and at home with yourself.
Initially, I was not without fear. Gauging the state of both the horse and the human is a gradual process. It does help to do other things with the horse before riding. Horses really know how to connect. I so want to be in harmony,

and I have found horses to be really helpful in that process. My experience with horses is not extensive, but it changed the way I feel about myself. Horses are loving and intuitive beings, and I have found myself having more love and intuition around them. Horses are not only intuitive, loving, and intelligent; they are also really masterful, stoic transportation.

I must say, riding is so much fun. I love riding. I feel that riding is like galloping hastily out of my own long-standing troubles. I feel free on the horse's back. I feel lighter and more competent. It is as if the horse carries my load. Connecting with a horse is not an easy process.

My really good teacher Mr. Bach was very helpful in that delicate task. He knew it was important to feel what the horse was able to do at any given moment. Horses don't align through force. Really, neither do I. For me, no-force is paramount to my success. Horses are very real and authentic creatures. It has to be a partnership between humans and horses. Horses need to feel safe and respected. I need that same safety and respect.

The horse that I am familiar with is Otis. The initial moments in getting to know Otis always started with hanging out in his stable. We would brush him and fix his stall, gauging his state and my mood before taking it to the next level. Then, Mr. Bach would have me climb up on the horse and ride to the pasture. There, we would start the main lesson. All we did was ride around in a circle. My experience of being fully on the horse was so liberating.

Horses help me let go of my thoughts of needing things to be in a specific way. I then connect with who I really am. Patient and free. Being in harmony is such an awesome feeling of space and love. Riding helps me go beyond my thought processes and feel free.

Horses have such a unique ability to transmit empathy. They say individuals on the spectrum have trouble with empathy. I have not found that to be true about you at all. What are your thoughts on this?

Being empathic has nothing to do with being on the spectrum or not.

What do you think being empathic entails? Some say that when you have a lot of empathy that allows you to see beyond what is tangible, you are an empath. Would you say you are one? If so, how would you define it?

I am so tuned into real emotion. I think what people feel is so often not congruent with what they say they feel. I am an empath. I must often clear out other people's energy. I mostly let it go when I sleep. I see being sensitive as incredibly important, in that many individuals don't know what they are experiencing. I think my empathic ability is a resource. I tune into people's energy by how it feels in their presence. It is so important to tune in. I think many people are very inconsistent in tuning in with themselves.

How do you mean?

Seeing how centered I can be when I am doing well makes me feel that anything is possible. Tension arises when one is not being tuned into oneself. The needy part of a person is failing to tune in because it is occupied with tuning out.

In tuning into other people, we sometimes abandon ourselves.

We have talked about a sense of being home, the experience of universal consciousness, a feeling of exuberance and freedom, music and animals, and empathy as one important aspect of alignment. What else is there to be said about being in harmony with ourselves and others?
I think the most important thing is to be in ongoing connection with one's soul. Our soul is not troubled. Our soul is not afraid. Our soul has no need to surpass others, to compete, to conquer. I think the more we connect with our soul—the seeing, loving soul—the more we see the beauty of this life.

What else in your life helps you connect with beauty and well-being?
I love to hike.

We do a lot of that. What is helpful about hiking?
I really love Mother Nature. Real nature is healing my OCD. I need to be inside a forest antenna twice a day.

I'm not sure I understand the antenna thing . . .
I see the trees as my antennae to the soul. I see the earth as my home. I am so lucky to be able to spend so much time in nature.

Lina, I have always thought that one thing that is amazing about you is that you keep undergoing constant transformations. Like the Greek philosopher Heraclitus said: "No man ever steps in the same river twice, for it is not the same river and he is not the same man."
I am never stagnant. I try at all times to allow myself to yearn for new challenges.

If it's true that we have various gifts that we are meant to use for the benefit of those around us, can you tell me about yours?
Seeing in the dark is my gift. Seeing the light in the darkest night. I need to see in the dark because I'm often there. I am often stuck in the space of ambivalent OCD and tedious anxiety. I have to always center on the light, amicably and tenaciously.

You once spelled something about how you are trying to "eradicate density." What did you mean by this? Were you talking about density within or outside of yourself?
I meant density of thought inside myself.

What does a dense thought look like for you?
A thought that centers around an OCD, or an extremely sadistic thought.

Does the extremely sadistic thought come from the frustrations of autism, or from somewhere else?
It comes from not being able to express myself verbally.

I can only imagine the frustration. When we were out hiking the other day, you spelled something about deities. . . . Why are you laughing?
I'm laughing at your intensity.

Okay, fair enough. And what about deities? Are they funny?
Incredibly. I think laughing is a serious remedy for density. And yes, I am talking about earth

fairies and angels. Deities on earth helping us with density. To be honest, I am tentative about talking about deities. I am in such an aligned place and don't want anything to disturb that.

Love that. You are protective of your own happiness and your own calm. At one point you spelled that you were in an "oracle mood." What does that mood feel like?
It feels so alive.

Do angels and earth fairies help you with seeing things, being in "an oracle mood," having perspective, becoming less dense, etc.?
Entities can be friendly or not friendly. I am into the friendly ones; they are so incredibly friendly and aligned in a loving way.

Can anyone be connected with them?
I think so. It's a matter of having a receptive mind.

When you connect with all that, it seems to lighten things up.
I think Source is full of laughter, which also helps me master a love for my clan on this earth.

What clan?

Need I explain that? I mean my family and my friends. I am always aware that I chose this. It's a calling to help you and my dad. I always felt that you guys are my responsibility.

What do I need help with?

I think you need help with seeing how it can always be healing to be here on this planet. I think you are in the other dimensions a lot. I think you long for your aligned tribe.

So, what do I do with that?

Mom, it's not a question of doing, it's about inhaling this life.

What will happen if I inhale this life?

I don't really know, but I think you will align with your tribe. I think you will stop longing for the other dimensions.

That's awesome.

Yes—I so am love, not hate. Love is the answer to everything.

What are you here to help your dad with?
I am here to help my dad in this dimension. My real mission is to help Mom. Mom, I am your mastery of love. I teach you reality beyond this reality. By loving Mom through enough mastery of beyond-experience that she can act on her greatest moments of alignment.

When you say this, it almost sounds like you and some higher power are talking about me.
Yes, I am always talking with my real soul. It's not that I have a plan so much as that I *am* the plan. There is so much that I have to love—it's insurmountable. In the past I have always washed the real me away. I am not interested in doing that anymore.

Can you tell me more about washing your real you away?
I hid behind my symptoms of autism. It radically changed when I seized the moment after having nearly died.

You have nearly died twice. Which experience led to this radical change?
I meant the hospitalization [with diabetic ketoacidosis]. All I can say is that I saw how having time here on this earth is a lovely thing, and I wanted to treat it with all my mastery and reverence.

What about the other near-death experience, when we almost drowned at Fire Island?
I don't remember that.

We were on the beach on a really stormy day and standing in the water only up to our knees. Then, suddenly, we were just swept away, far from the beach. I still don't know how it could have happened. I tried to help you swim back and you got really scared and pushed me away. I think you saw how scared I was and panicked. We were so far out that it seemed futile. I felt so strongly that we were not done yet, it was not our time. The water was black and seemed so vast. It was the most vulnerable moment of my life. And then somehow we came back, not because I saved us or anything; that

would have been impossible. As powerful as the current had been that took us out there, it brought us back. We could feel the bottom of the ocean again. There was a lady right at the water's edge and I was so tired I could hardly drag us up on the beach. She helped us. We lay in the sand in the sun for a long time.
[Lina smiles]

You're smiling?
In so many ways, we have had a really rough ride.

Tell me about it.
I think it's a little funny that we almost drowned. I think we almost drowned in so many different universal ways.

It does feel like a lot of near-death experiences. What do you think about the impact of all these excruciating and often frightening and overwhelming events?
I think it made me see how I can survive a lot of hardship.

You seem to be able to survive almost anything. What's your secret?
Is real surviving seeing beyond the hardship?

I think so; what are your thoughts?
I think surviving takes genuine strength, and I also think it takes a faith in something beyond the alienating challenge.

Do you feel that you have this faith? And how would you describe that "something beyond"?
In my life I have trust in a love that doesn't stop, that's totally attuned with my needs, that's nesting inside me at all times.

CHAPTER FIVE

On Communication

I Am Soaring

In real life I am a soaring eagle.
Need I always indicate the soaring truth?
Is my life a tentative talking tedious
    ageless havoc?
All I am is a loving eagle without wings.
I am ahead of pestering people.
I am ahead of ignorance.
I am ahead of seeing yearnings without end.

—Lina H. Lyons

In learning how to spell my thoughts, I saw my life sending me forward. I saw my life having pertinent meaning. I became aware of how I can share what I have seen in this world and many other worlds. In my life, I am always in between worlds. My spelling can help me be here on this planet. I can realize my thoughts. I can wander here with others. I can be a human who is understood and who understands.

Do you remember what it was like when you didn't have communication? You've written about what it was like to lose your expressive speech, but what about all the years between then and now?

I do remember it was jarring and alienating. I always felt alone. It was so difficult not to be able to align with others and to be so isolated inside myself. I meandered into scary places. I had no way of getting out on my own. The breakdowns were always my way of trying to get out of my own thoughts.

Lina, you almost never have those terrible breakdowns anymore.
I am now so able to talk about my thoughts, and it helps me so much.

You wrote a little bit about what it was like to begin to spell with Jane and then with me. Around that time, you also worked directly with Soma [Mukhopadhyay]. *Can you tell me more about what was it like be able to use words to express who you are inside for the first time?*
I was beside myself with excitement. It was like coming out of a no-man's-land. It was like being led into my central communication.

Is this really hard to describe?
It is. I have no real words to describe how all this affected me. It was like coming into all my opportunities. It was like seeing the sacred sun for the first time.

Wow. What was the first thing you wanted to say to everyone around you? Was there a first thing? Was it hard to decide what to say first?
To be honest, I just wanted to say all that I hadn't been able to say.

What did you think of all our reactions to your expressions—some of us crying, some speechless, wide-eyed, exhilarated . . . ?
It was all in the really happy realm.

With Jane, you very quickly got into interesting philosophical discussions; talks about religion, poetry, and all kinds of stuff. Any thoughts about that period? There was so much inspiration and also so much anxiety.
It was unbelievably difficult beneath every word. I was always thinking of myself as not smart, and suddenly I realized I was very smart.

So, you had to reevaluate everything.
Yes, I had to totally accept a new reality.

What made you able to do it?

I so wanted to be heard and not be considered a crazy wild maniac.

Is that really what you imagined the people in your life thought of you?

I always thought all of the wildness was my fault.

What do you think about that now?

I think it was just frustration about not being able to communicate.

Lina, before—when you were not able to use the letter boards to make yourself understood—people around you talked about *you rather than* with *you quite a bit. That still happens a lot. How do you feel when people talk about you in the third person?*

I feel like my identity is erased. I don't align so much with having lost out on things, but rather I am a product of what I have been through, and I am happy.

Can you tell me more about what it has been like to communicate on letter boards? It hasn't been entirely easy . . .
I am so insecure about other people's wishes to know me.

You have seen a lot of other people's difficulties in welcoming your true thoughts.
I don't understand it. I anticipated people being happy. I thought they would be incredibly tuned into me.

That has been so disappointing. Where does it leave you when you don't feel that people are tuned into your mode of communication?
I am not super happy about it. It feels like a density that I can't do anything about.

Where do you think this comes from? What makes it hard for people to get with the program?
I'm not sure, maybe they need things to stay the same.

You mean other people need to relate to you the same way as they always have?
I mean people have trouble believing that I am an intelligent person.

Is there anything else you want to say about this?
I am willing to not take this personally.

That's beautiful. Spelling in itself isn't easy. What do you think makes it so tricky for you, as well as for the people assisting you, to communicate on the letter board?
For me, aligning with my true thoughts is really difficult. Density is in the way. I think part of the difficulty is not having the words to describe what I know. It's a constant seeing without having the right words to describe what I see. I see in color and energy, not in concepts and words. I see in sensations, not the forms. My words are incredibly tedious compared to what I know. Seeing so much more, I feel defeated in trying to find words.

That reminds me of what Malidoma [Patrice Somé] *writes in his book* The Healing Wisdom of Africa *about the views of the Dagara, the indigenous group that he belonged to. The Dagara consider trees and plants to be the most intelligent beings, because they don't need words to communicate and therefore live closer to the intrinsic meaning of language. Malidoma writes about how, for his people, to "utter"—to speak with words—signifies a nostalgia for and an exile from our true home. Where does letter board spelling fit in this reasoning? Is spelling some kind of compromise between being home and being in exile? Or how do you see it?*

I think spelling is different from talking. It's easier to align with Source in pointing to letters. I think it's important to be able to share our inner worlds. I also think letter board spelling helps us to connect with this world. This world is beautiful, and I want to energetically transform myself in order to really be here.

So, for you, it's more about really being here on earth; you are already connected spiritually. This seems *somewhat related to what Malidoma says about the Dagara people, who—so comfortable and versatile in the spiritual realm—"may have forgotten to integrate with matter."* You also know a lot about other realms; but this realm, this earth, is difficult to integrate with. And that seems to be true for a lot of folks on the spectrum?*

I think that's true. I think all people on the spectrum have trouble being here. I have trouble, too, but nature helps me so much. In nature, I feel like I can be here. I see how you are trying to understand autism. I think you are onto something.

I think Malidoma was onto something, is onto something.

I think you and Malidoma are onto something. I am trying to take healing from Nature. I'm beginning to feel at home on this planet.

---

* Somé, Malidoma Patrice, *The Healing Wisdom of Africa: Finding Life Purpose Through Nature, Ritual, and Community* (Jeremy P. Tarcher/Putnam, 1998), 29.

I think I'm beginning to feel at home here too.
I see how aligned you are with nature, and it inspires me to find my home.

You inspire me to find my home.
I think we will find our home. I see myself being at home.

How does spelling connect with the issue of finding home?
I think spelling—expressing my true thoughts—is the way I can feel more at home here on earth.

How do you feel that your life has changed over the years since you learned to spell?
I must say, it took a while for me to realize that I could have a meaningful life. I could let my family and friends get to know me. I began to understand that I can entirely take an active part in my life. I wanted to have a chance to talk about myself and not just be a target for others' thoughts about who I am. My self-esteem transformed. I felt that I was capable of deciding

things for myself. I saw a sincere yearning to really understand me in you, Mom, and in my sister, too. I saw how I can study and learn new things and began to internalize a sense of myself as a lovely young woman. I think all the most important things in my life came from spelling.

It is the best thing ever. And at the same time, you have often said that in some sense, communicating on letter boards is next to impossible. What happens to us when we do the impossible?
To be honest, it is still impossible. I think we have to rely not on ourselves, but on our Source.

You know what Muhammad Ali said . . .
Impossible is nothing.

CHAPTER SIX

An Ideal Education

She who reconciles the ill-matched threads
of her life, and weaves them gratefully
into a single cloth—
it's she who drives the loudmouths from
the hall
and clears it for a different celebration

—Rainer Maria Rilke*

---

* Rainer Maria Rilke, *Rilke's Book of Hours: Love Poems to God,* trans. Anita Barrows and Joanna Macy (Riverhead Books, 2005), I, 17.

Being someone who doesn't talk, I have found that education is not an easy thing for me to come by. I have heard my mother speak to different directors of various schools about how I need an age-appropriate, not infantilizing, education—to no avail. I have tried a lot of different schools. My having so much OCD makes it hard for teachers to allow me a good education. In the autism community, there is a lot of focus on behaviors, even though my behaviors are less intrusive when my mind is busy with academic studies. My desire is for all students to have a real education. I don't understand what part of wanting a real education is so challenging for most people to get. In the last day program I attended, the focus was on utilizing sports, having Ping-Pong tournaments, throwing fastballs, biking, and running on a treadmill. Many of my teachers wanted to change my behaviors, but not being able to study makes my behaviors worse.

I am a little wary of communicating too much with people I don't know. With my incredible anxiety, I worry that people don't believe that it's my own thoughts I'm expressing. I don't want to deal with other people's doubts. In a different school, I had some weary experiences of teachers not believing in the method of communication that I am using. It was very difficult to express my thoughts when they didn't believe the thoughts were mine. In the middle of the summer session, they stopped trying to facilitate. I think they were going to evaluate whether to continue with spelling. For a long time, I didn't have a school; I had to amicably depart from that one, since I couldn't communicate my real thoughts.

Having an education is something I have wanted for many alienating years. I wanted to study things, subjects—not just reiterated and incredibly boring facts, like how to celebrate Thanksgiving and Christmas. I am so tired of talking about facts that I don't care about. In the center of the world are really interesting things. I have discovered how my lineage is really feisty. I am a Viking, and I can conquer pretty much any hardship. I read the Norse myths and found my own yearning for adventure. I wanted to be like Thor in his super strong talents and courage. I wanted to be like Freya in seeing possibility and making her life salient with passion.

In the fall of 2024, I audited an English class at Amherst, where my sister goes to college. In this experience I found incredible real soaring inspiration, and a sense of connection in studying tenuously with others. All I can say is that I see how rich my life can be. I also see how centered I can feel when I devote myself to my work; when I use my brain; when I utilize myself in understanding a lot of different characters in the stories, songs and poems I have seen and heard about. To meet myself in this way, as someone who can study and complete homework, is a whole new level for me. Being a person who cannot speak, I have found that I can still study, I can still learn, I still have a good mind.

* * *

Lina, who are you as a student?
I always allocate my resources between talking on the board and thinking inside.

What's the implication of such . . . shall we say . . . dual focus?
It's a really difficult journey to want a decent education centered on depth while also channeling my spiritual inclination. I always want to study, but there are not enough teachers who can do the RPM [Rapid Prompting Method, a mode of facilitating spelling/typing] with me.

I hear you. It's been one long quest to find teachers who are also facilitators and who can teach you on a level that matches your educational needs.
It's been incredibly frustrating.

Most of the time, you end up being stuck with me. And most people your age just don't want to study with their mother. But at the same time, I guess it is what it is.
It is a lot to ask for you to always study with me. I see how happy you are for me when I do it with someone else.

I love it when your life expands and includes communication with others as well. At the same time, I love to study with you. I can feel how focused and committed you are.

I am super focused now. I have done so much willing work to score well on the placement test for [Passaic Community] college, and I am very proud of how entirely well it went.

It was incredible. You were so determined: sitting for four hours in front of the computer, just all in; carefully considering and answering everything; writing your essay. I don't think you have ever taken this kind of test before.

I have never done anything like that before. I already feel that I'm available for my studies in a transformative way.

And now you are taking community college classes at Passaic. Sociology was the first class. Any thoughts about how that went?

I loved it so much. It incredibly jolted my sense of society and transformed me into someone who is more aware of inequalities in America. I feel that I really want to work towards change. I took Sociology 101 and ended up feeling that America needs to call 911 on its politics. I see how ignorant most of us are of the suffering of others. I tuned into the reality of others and will never again forget it. I am so happy to have had this experience, though it was very difficult to stay in class. I was the only student with autism; and the person going with me at first didn't know how to facilitate spelling, which watered down my enthusiasm. But I loved to study at home, and I mastered every assignment. I also think that my professor had a lovely, inclusive flexibility; he really was the reason I could do this. I so love this professor, and I am so happy to have had him as my teacher. I am really looking forward to more classes, and I hope my next professor will be as lovely as this one.

And as if that's not enough, we have discovered a whole new community of individuals on the spectrum (and their families) in our own area.

I see how deities have conspired to make this happen.

It sure feels like it.

I called on them to help us when we left my last day program. In being released from a past that didn't serve me, I was freed to have something new.

I love how it seems like life always restores balance. We were actually kicked out of that school. Why do you think that happened?

I think I said too much to the teachers about not being happy. I think they sensed that this was not a good place for me. Mom, you also caused the ending by telling the teacher to stop yelling at a student who was so upset that he ended up on the floor. I see how you can't abolish your thoughts when someone is in trouble.

What do you make of the fact that the director of the program then reached out asking you to come back?

I think he so regretted his angry need to control everything. To be honest, I don't ever want to be in a day program again.

I think those days have passed. Like you said before, this whole process seems so ingeniously guided.
I think it's all in the realm of universal initiation. I think we are in the realm of Source. I see how we are moving into the realm of possibility.

It does seem like everything is opening up for you. I know how happy it makes you to be able to hear good literature, to analyze a book or an idea, to write a poem or story, to learn and study and have access to interesting material. . . . And yet, it has been so hard for us to find an educational setting that can satisfy your needs as a student.
All I can say is that it's a yearning that won't go away.

What do you think needs to happen in our society—within our educational systems; in schools for autism; in the attitudes of legislators, special needs teachers, speech pathologists, etc.—to allow you the age-appropriate education that you long for?
I think it's entirely up to all officials to understand that people on the spectrum are not intellectually challenged.

Appropriate education is kind of a basic human right, isn't it?
It's a basic human need!

Will you keep fighting for your own right to have an appropriate education?
I will always fight for this to become reality.

We have read various works of classic literature: Their Eyes Were Watching God, The Grapes of Wrath, Women Who Run with the Wolves, *etc. What is it like for you to be exposed to these kinds of books?*
It's a whole new world for me to connect with these incredible authors. They show me how I can widen my vision in my own life. When I hear these texts, I am inspired and new in my own thoughts.

Wow. Lina, when we first started reading more age-appropriate books, it was hard. What changed? What advice can you offer to teachers, parents, or individuals

on the spectrum who may struggle in the beginning of getting used to reading (or listening to reading)?
I think just hang in there—you will enjoy it sooner than you think.

How do you think hearing great literature impacts your own language?
I think it's central in helping me distance myself from OCD and deal more effectively with my anxiety.

I know you're interested in literature; what other academic subjects are you drawn to?
I am drawn to all subjects.

Considering the challenges that you find yourself with, what would be an ideal educational setting for you? What kind of circumstances would allow you the college experience that you want?
I think a regular college would be ideal, but it is very difficult for me to be in a centered space. I really would like to keep going to college, but it is very hard.

What would make it easier?
If I had much less OCD and anxiety, things would be much easier.

Do you think that what you were working on in your previous program in New Jersey—lots of movement, opening up motor pathways, making your body do what you want, becoming more intentional in your physical movements—was helpful, or a waste of time?
I think it was helpful but not enough.

What would have made it better?
If more studies were incorporated, it would have been more satisfactory.

And by studies, you mean . . .?
More academic studies.

What would you like to say to school administrators and teachers at special needs programs who believe that they have to address behaviors before introducing academic studies?
I think academic studies make behaviors go away.

Why do you think this is so hard for people running schools to understand? What's in the way?
I think what's in the way is that they have always done it in that old way.

Do you think this book could help make education accessible for people on the spectrum?
I think so, if the right people read it. It may help them understand that individuals on the spectrum have no problem with intellectual capacity.

CHAPTER SEVEN

Words of Advice to People on the Sidelines

Lullabies

In so many needy ways
I always want a lullaby life
I always need a love that
sings soothing songs for me

I realize it's not a love
that satiates me that is a good love
not a love that caters to my every need
that I really need

I see myself in the soothing song
hollering and making noise
is also me

Seeing my songs changing in the wind
talking to me about nothing but
tones and yearning

Centered in myself
I don't need another lullaby.

—Lina H. Lyons

I think the most helpful way to advise people who have someone on the spectrum in their lives is to describe my own family's process. In December of 2025, I had a lot of difficulties again. My mother is a lot of things to me, and I saw how tired she became. I saw how she couldn't have this life anymore. In Mom, I saw how I needed to change my ways. I think my mom was beginning to go a little nuts. She kept telling me I had to relate to her as a human being, not a servant. I harbored a lot of tedious entitlement. I had to look at it. It was difficult.

It was super difficult for me too. I hate challenging the OCD and asking you to do things that are difficult for you, like washing the dishes or hanging your jacket on a hanger or not saying "yes, yes, yes," all the time. I think it's because I'm never very confident that I will win, that it will work, that we can both change our ways—you doing more, me doing less.

I think it's really hard seeing myself as entitled. I see how I expect you to do things for me. I see how I act all helpless, and how you are entirely tired of it.

Yeah, it's true; and I'm not really very good at insisting that you do more, unless I'm irritated or angry enough to give myself permission to ask.

I think that is so true, and it's harder for me to do stuff when you are mad.

I totally get that.

Is my being helpless a big deal?

I think so. I think it's not the truth. It's just something we have created because you've had so much suffering and so many challenges. Even if we have acknowledged that you are competent and capable, we have often failed to act on that awareness.

I think having you as my mother is a little confusing. I have a lot of ambivalence about being capable, and so do you!

For real; we have been colluding in ways that have held both of us back.

I think there is only one way to resolve this: halting the helplessness and tentative seeing of my power.

Agreed. And for me to expect more from you; and for you to see me not just as a mother, but as a person, too.

Is a lot of seeing of each other the solution? I think so. All I can say is that I want this to change.

Remember when you said to me that all I talked about were my needs?
Mom, I do remember. You just couldn't stop lecturing me about everything I had done wrong.

Yeah, I wasn't super fun to be with. But I'm glad I finally got it, however imperfectly; I got that I actually have to stand up for my own needs. I have to fight—not just for you, but for me, too.
I so align with that. I see how much closer we are now.

What are you thinking about now?
I think about how I have always seen this but wasn't able to say it. I see how horrendous my OCD is to you, and I'm calling you to stand up against it.

I think if I did that ongoingly it wouldn't suddenly overwhelm me, and I wouldn't suddenly explode out of frustration. I don't know why I can't give myself permission to set a boundary unless I am at my wits' end.
I align with that frustration, and I'm always

okay with you saying the stuff you're saying about it.

So much power in being real.
I think authenticity is a lifesaver.

Well, you are a really accepting human being. At the same time, there was a moment there when we both were very tired of each other.
I was so tired of you, and I thought it was not possible for us to change.

Yes, I felt very hopeless as well. It is hard to see these kinds of things in a defenseless kind of way. But I think that process may have been the most important thing we have ever done together.
I think if we hadn't done that we wouldn't have made it. I see how close we are now. I see how we are tentatively a lot more Zen. How I already am so much more in charge of myself. When you work to have it seen that you are human, I feel your humanity too. And your individuality. I see our equality as well.

It's amazing how much easier everything is now. I don't use a whole lot of energy to hold back my reactions to various things. I just speak up right away, and you seem to really like that.

I like to get many chances to do better. I say that I want to be an equal, but inside I am ambivalent. I tend to go back and forth a lot. I say I want to do more independent things, but I'm often more interested in being cared for.

Yes, I have noticed that, and I appreciate your honesty about it. The difference now, though, is that I'm onto you. I have worked through some of my ambivalence about being on your case.

I see a lot more alignment in you when you say what you want, even when it's challenging.

Yes, and it seems like you respond better to more consistent challenges. Is that true?

Yes, I love being challenged. But I also would like to have a less troubled family.

Would you care to elaborate on that?
I think it has to do with the idea of love in my broken-up family. It's hard for me to be direct in my communication with my family. I see how difficult it is for my parents to communicate, and I call on you guys to talk to each other.

Yes, I have noticed that. How do you see yourself doing that, calling on us to communicate? If we could learn to do that better, how would that help you?
I do it by being difficult and forcing you guys to talk about it. I feel that I cannot be direct and integrated if you fail to have honest and straightforward conversations.

I think that's fair. Isn't it a bit related to the life-death-life cycle that Clarissa Pinkola Estés writes about? It's so hard to hold onto a relationship when it gets difficult.*
I think it's a lot like that, and what comes out of

* The concept of the life-death-life cycle comes from Estés's 1992 bestseller, *Women Who Run with the Wolves: Myths and Stories of the Wild Woman Archetype.* Estés encourages us to search our relationships and our psyche for elements that have to "die" in order to allow for new life.

the death part is a new life. In so many ways, death is no different from life. Allowing death is illuminating it. I am in a life-death alignment. I am in a seeing place.

* * *

Centering on my independence is very important. I'm really invested in my own freedom and space. Having the space to create my own life, having the freedom to do my own thing, having people in my life other than my family, expressing my own thoughts—these things are everything to me. It's a less amicable path, in that I have to rebel against the people who have influence over me and do not understand who I am. I also have to rebel against the people who I love the most. I have to find myself. I have to walk my own intrepid road. I have no idea how, but I know I have to. It helps me so much when people see me and treat me as an equal. I see how I can independently make choices about my studies, my style of clothing, my living situation, my relationships. Having to be dependent on others to an incredible degree makes this almost impossible. Gauging what I want is part of it. I also need to have a chance to create my own mastery, from washing my own dishes, to making my own bed, to making choices about what I eat, to deciding what I do in my daily life.

I think I can stand my own ground. The other day we went to a party. I saw an old teacher and she came up to me to have a conversation about my stylish hat. I needed to say something, because she talked to me as if no time had passed since the time when I was her student. It was a time when I wasn't spelling on the letter boards, and no one knew how to relate to me. At this party, I spelled to my old teacher, "I aligned with you even though you didn't know how smart I was." It was incredibly cathartic to be able to say that. I saw how I can stand my ground and assert myself. At that same party, there was a mother who related to her son as if he were her lover. It was so disturbing; I wanted to talk to her about trespassing his boundaries.

I felt so tedious about it and I wanted to leave. It was not a good scene. I think it's very difficult for parents and caretakers to know when to give physical input and when to give space. It takes a lot of sensitivity to know when to tend to someone's lack of body awareness and when to let them master themselves.

In my life, I appreciate everyone who includes me as a person in my own right. I am so different from most people, but I think it's universally important to encourage diversity. It is the radical way we connect with each other. I really benefit from an inclusive stance. When I feel welcomed and included, I thrive. In a less inclusive environment, I always shrink. It is of such importance that we share each other's burdens. In sharing what we struggle with, we find that we are not that different.

Having autism, I am often excluded from so many opportunities: schools, jobs, theater and music lessons; real romance and lovely friendships. I want to be less excluded, but it's a lot worse for me to try and fail to be included than to not try. For example, I am very afraid of failing my college studies, but I am willing to try because I really want to study.

I feel I have failed so many things; I have messed up many parties, trips, communication lessons, intolerable treatments. I want to keep trying, but it is almost impossible to find the confidence. I see diversity as something that benefits not only me, but all people. Amicably allowing all voices to be heard and seeing how we are not so different opens us up to new people, new learning, new experiences.

There are many ways for others to be sensitive to someone who doesn't speak. Talking about me in the third person leaves me in the outsider realm. I am tired of being on the outside. There is simply no wearier place for me than on the outside of my own life.

In conversation, when I'm speaking on letter boards, I often find that people turn to my facilitator rather than to me. It's horrendously frustrating, because I'm right there. I want to be involved. This is the most irritating thing ever. I have no way of asserting myself other than pointing to a letter board, channeling my thoughts through my hand—and I need receptivity to do it. Why are people talking to my mother when I'm standing right there? It's a less aware thing, a kind of ignorance. I really enjoy talking to people. I'm actually much more social than my mother, so it's a little weird that she gets to talk and I have to listen. She tries to move the conversation to include me, but sometimes people keep on addressing her. I think it comes from insecurity, and I understand—but I really have to desensitize myself to open up, and I hope this will improve. It takes a lot of courage to speak my thoughts. I mastered my already rusty murals in spelling in order to be here, to be seen and heard. I mean that I need to have murals, or visual images, inside myself in order to spell anything. I so already have seen hastening of my festive seeing.

In my life, I'm always at someone's mercy. I'm always dependent on others to give me a chance to insinuate my own decisions. I'm tired of living in this way. I want to be my own master. I want to lead my own life. My entire rusty, havoc-afflicted life. It doesn't have to be perfect; it has to be mine. I see not a lost life but a found life. I see not an unreal life but a life that harvests so centered a love that nothing can stop me. I'm ready, I'm here, I'm real and true. I don't care where I have my house, I care where I have my heart. I want to encourage everyone in my life to let me live and learn and fail and succeed. I really want to lead my own life as much as possible.

I realized recently that I want to live in my own place with friends. I see this as a positive development, and I think I will make it happen. I love to live in my parents' houses, but I am an adult and I think I need more independence. I'm hoping that I can go back and forth between my mom's house and my dad's house and my own house; I want to see how that goes. I have never been away for very long from my mom. I see it as hard; but I think it will also be fun. I see it as really important to have incremental changes in one's life. To implement tiny changes that eventually lead to bigger transformation. I have faith that I am guided and supported by Source and by my family.

Setting boundaries is a really important thing. Because of autism, I have a lot of trouble with this. By setting boundaries I mean talking about what I want and need, about what is okay with me and what isn't. Today I set a boundary about not writing cards to my father and my sister. It's my father's birthday tomorrow, and my sister is coming home after a long trip abroad. I never thought it was a good idea to write to my sister. I think it's really awkward to write a card to one's sister. Mom thought that I should be thinking about my sister, that it would be a generous thing. But I just didn't see it, and I stood my ground. I so love my mom's passion, but it's important to me that I do what I think is best. When it comes to writing a birthday card to my father, I want to communicate directly with him (not with my mom facilitating). I stood my ground there too and will bring a blank card to him. It's a little bit funny that I'm bringing a blank card, but this is my decision and I'm sticking to it.

I also think respecting boundaries is one of the most important things for others to remember to do. Most people don't act as if I have sovereignty. They assume someone else has the power to decide over me. Having autism doesn't mean I have poor judgment. I have very good judgment, and I know how to make decisions about my own life. I know what I want to study, what I want to eat, who I want to hang out with, what supplements and treatments work for me. I already have a clear direction in my life, and I am sure of my own ability to realize my goals. I see no reason why anyone else should interfere. I really wish I could talk, because it would solve most of my problems. I see how many people suspect that the words I spell are not my words. I realized this when, as I mention in the chapter on education, I went to a school where half the teachers didn't believe that my spelling was my own. My mom and I decided to not have me continue there; my spelling was compromised because of the lack of trust in my integrity. It was a very sad experience, because I loved my friends and my teachers. But my voice was more important than the losses I had to endure. I don't regret leaving, and I have found a community where my already wonderful thoughts are believed. I don't ever have to prove myself. I don't have to be seen as insidious and unintelligent. I can make jokes and be silly and be smart and people trust that the words I use are my own. I love myself so much, and I want to be loved for who I am.

People on the spectrum also need not to have to process the seedy thoughts and feelings of others. I don't often see a lovely inside reality in the thoughts and emotions I tap into. Instead, it's feelings that can't be talked about. It's a lot of things that people don't want to accept about themselves. I see it and I try to help, but it often has an effect on me. It has made many of my days a living hell. I have tried to process all matters related to genuine deities. I have also tried to help people see more aspects of themselves. I am so busy trying to process the rejected feelings of others that I have no energy left to process my own. I am so inundated by the inner lives of others that there is no space left for my own internal reality. In many situations, people are too happy feeling transformed in their lives to realize that they need to acknowledge their own insidiousness in order to heal.

I see how I need to claim my inner space a lot more than I do now. I want to discern what's mine and what's someone else's. It helps me when others process their weary emotions. I need so much space and clarity in people around me. I think this is true for anyone with serious autism. It's also important for me to respect the boundaries of others. I want to consider the needs and feelings of others too, and master my own anger and frustration in this life. I have trouble with that because I unify, bordering on symbiotic enmeshment in so many situations. Having autism is hellish in so many ways. It is like being exposed to all human emotion on this planet. I see separation and integrity as the solution. The most helpful thing anyone can do to support a person on the spectrum is to have good boundaries. To know what is theirs and what belongs to others. To be centered and honest and not take things personally. To feel the need to heal, look at themselves mostly, and not judge too harshly. In many situations, a person's love of their work with autistic individuals is greater than their love for the person they are helping. This has devastating consequences. I think the poem below, "Genuine Sadness," expresses incredible alienation about people harvesting others. I think it expresses how I feel about people's insane need for acknowledgment and glory.

Genuine Sadness

Density is all around
Interacting maliciously already happened
Insurance from enmeshment already
    already already has camouflaged in
    sinister ways

Dense is my soul
Dense is my heart
Dense is my mind

Halos and crosses have seen their sun
Halos and crosses have seen their moon
Insurance from mastery has already
already already gone anticipating
meandering hostile feelings

Dense is my soul
Dense is my heart
Dense is my mind

—Lina H. Lyons

AFTERWORD

Healing Myself

A Love Meaning to Burst

I so think a love meaning to burst
is a love meaning to level
with all that is real.
I think a love meaning to burst
is a love meaning to test
our insensitive souls.
I think a love meaning to burst

is alive and meaning to indiffer[*] and react
and rearrange and resolve.

—Lina H. Lyons

* * *

Wanting to smile has a lot of meaning for me. I so often cannot harvest the very smile that is budding inside me. I smile inside all the time. It comes from a lovely sense of the comical aspects of life. I have a mother who sees my inside smiles. I want everyone to see my smiles and to comprehend my sense of humor. In this little story is my mother insisting that life is more funny than grim. I so love to laugh and smile.

The Really Happy Girl Who Never Smiled
She was happy but she never showed it.
She saw the people laughing but she never
joined them.

---

* A word I invented.

The people tried to make her laugh but to
no avail. It was futile.
Neither her sister or her brother, her
mother or her father, could entice this
girl to smile.
The parents tried to have a teacher come
and teach the girl to smile.
The brother and the sister tried to have
their camaraderies* come and make
her smile.
She would not even move her mouth.
She was as serious as antique furniture.
She wanted to smile so bad, but nothing or
no one could help her.
That was until her lovely, bent-over mom
saw her tedious face and thought it
was so grim and grumpy that she
broke out in a roaring laughter. She
laughed so hard she almost died.
And as the girl watched her mother, she
smiled.

---

* Or "loves."

* * *

Having autism is a lot harder than having a regular human life. I see my feelings as either totally overwhelming or not there at all. When tensions arise, I shut down. Then, when I try to feel something, I want to get away from my unbearable emotions. It's very hard to win. The transformation that I am looking for is almost impossible to find. I search every day for the most transformative insights. I search for the light in everything I experience. I try to look for the truth in the middle of my greatest fear. Need I love myself more? The truth is, I don't always know how to love myself. I don't always know how to care for myself. I often utilize my people for that task, but I need to utilize myself to do this. I want to heal myself. I want to be my own healer. I want to be my own navigator. I want to live my own life. I love the density on this planet, and I really think I called myself to this earth to learn how to live here in the most transformative way. I realize this when I sometimes get insidious and dark.

I have so much trouble with my emotions. I see how I can't do things for myself, and it hurts me. It hurts to be so dependent on others. It's so aggravating to always have to ask for help. It is so humiliating to be in that seat of dependency. I always want to be happy. I always want to connect with my real self. I need to overcome density. Everyone should lessen their density, but my density is a little extreme. Having autism is a race between density and bliss.

In dense thought, transformation is defeated. Talking about needing to have less dense thoughts brings more density. In thinking about what's not working, nothing works. Dense thought is preoccupied with needs and wants. Focusing on what one doesn't have makes it impossible to feel blissful. Having bliss is the same as having a clear and calm mind. Salient thoughts and peace are part of having real bliss. I state only what true bliss needs to be about. I don't have a lot of bliss; but when I do, I universally feel free. I have a deep connection with my Source. I am calling on my Source to help me heal myself.

In my life, I have had so much anxiety and OCD. So much anger. If I were to say something to my earlier self, I would tell myself not to give up. I would tell my earlier self not to be afraid. I'd tell myself that I really would come out of this hellish, alienating nest of anxiety and OCD. I really would experience a better life. Noticing how I can do better, I feel hopeful that others on the spectrum can, too. In transforming myself I can help others transform. In having a lovely life I believe that others can have a lovely life too. I see real mastery in myself and others. I have incredible hope for the autism community.

Truth is, my life has really changed. I have conquered a lot of my OCD and a lot of my anxieties. The main reason for my incredible progress is that I now can communicate. I can talk to the people in my life about what I think they need to accept and understand about me. I can study and advise about autism. I can have a life outside of autism's incarceration. I can talk to people about their issues and their need to heal themselves from their fear of living. I am so happy to have this way of connecting on this earth. This earth is a beautiful, incredibly intriguing nest for humans and animals and plants and waters and minerals. It is our home, and we need to care for it as if it were our closest friend. Anticipating our planet's needs and wants is no different from tending to ourselves. That is all I have to say in this book. That is all I have to say in this life, on this beautiful planet Earth.

A Past Realization

It's all right to align with artificial stencils.
It's all right to be seen aromatically.
It's all right to behead the hallowed alien.
It's all right to alienate the tedious alien.
It's all right to live in peace.
It's all right to feel seen by the fearful past.
It's all right to be in so masterful a love
on a left sensational sentiment.

—Lina H. Lyons